Watch It Grow
Sunflower
Barrie Watts

Smart Apple Media

First published in 2003 by Franklin Watts
96 Leonard Street, London EC2A 4XD, United Kingdom
Franklin Watts Australia, 56 O'Riordan Street, Alexandria, NSW 2015
Copyright © 2003 Barrie Watts

Editor: Jackie Hamley, Art director: Jonathan Hair,
Photographer: Barrie Watts, Reading consultant: Beverley Mathias

Published in the United States by Smart Apple Media
1980 Lookout Drive, North Mankato, Minnesota 56003

Library of Congress Cataloging-in-Publication Data

Watts, Barrie. Sunflower / Barrie Watts. p. cm. – (Watch it grow)
Summary: A simple introduction to how a sunflower grows from
seed to flowering plant.
ISBN 1-58340-232-2 1. Sunflowers–Life cycles–Juvenile literature.
[1. Sunflowers.] I. Title.
QK495.C74W35 2003 583'.99–dc21 2003042513

2 4 6 8 9 7 5 3 1

How to use this book

Watch It Grow has been specially designed to cater to a range
of reading and learning abilities. Initially children may just
follow the pictures. Ask them to describe in their own words
what they see. Other children will enjoy reading the single
sentence in large type in conjunction with the pictures. This
single sentence is then expanded in the main text. More adept
readers will be able to follow the text and pictures by them-
selves through to the conclusion of the sunflower's life cycle.

Contents

Sunflowers come from seeds.

Here is a sunflower seed. It is about half an inch (1.2 cm) long. It comes from the middle of a sunflower. The striped shell is hard and tough. It keeps the inside parts of the seed from drying out.

Inside the seed is a store of food that will be used to grow a new plant. During the winter, the seed is kept in a cool, dry place until it is ready to be planted.

The seed is planted.

In the spring, when the weather becomes warmer, the seed is planted in soil. The seed needs warmth and water to start to grow.

A week after planting, the shell of the seed has softened. Water from the soil goes through the shell. As it gets wet, the inside of the seed swells. The shell then splits open.

The seed grows roots.

Soon after the soft seed shell splits open, a tiny root pushes its way out.

The root grows down into the soil.
It collects water and **nutrients**,
which are sent back to the seed.

The seed leaves grow.

As the root sends water and **nutrients** back to the seed, the first leaves, called **seed leaves**, start to grow. They grow on top of a hollow tube called the stem.

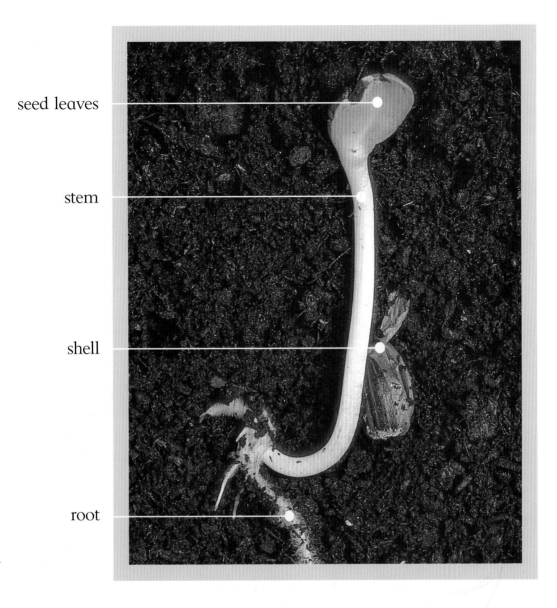

seed leaves

stem

shell

root

The **seed leaves** push their way to the surface of the soil. They are folded downward as they force their way up through the soil. This keeps them from getting damaged.

The seed leaves are big.

As soon as the **seed leaves** reach the surface of the soil, they unfold. They are oval and have a different shape than a normal leaf. The **seed leaves** use sunlight to start making food for the plant.

The food gives the plant the energy
it needs to grow. Now it can push
its roots deep into the soil. The
more roots the plant has, the more
water and **nutrients** it will get,
and the faster it will grow.

Larger leaves grow.

A week after the **seed leaves** appear, the sunflower plant's larger leaves start to grow. They grow up to a foot (30 cm) long and use sunlight to make even more food.

The large leaves have a network of thin, hollow tubes called **veins**. These **veins** carry food to the rest of the plant. When the large leaves have grown, the **seed leaves** are no longer needed. They turn yellow and dry up.

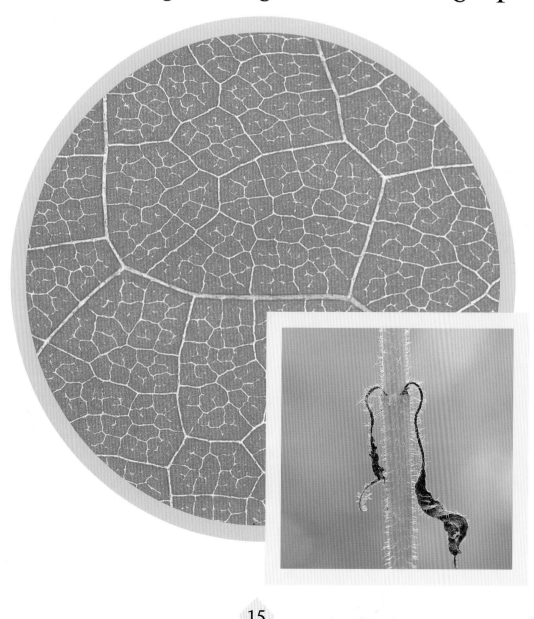

The stem is strong.

The stem
of the plant joins
the roots and the leaves. It is a tube
filled with soft, sponge-like **veins**
that carry food and water to the
other parts of the sunflower plant.

The stem can grow more than six feet (1.8 m) tall and is strong and flexible. It supports the plant as it grows and later supports its heavy flower.

The flower starts to grow.

After two months, the sunflower plant has grown several large leaves. These make lots of food so the plant can start to grow a flower bud.

The flower bud grows at the tip of the stem, where the newest leaves appear. At first, only the outer parts of the flower can be seen.

The flower bud is big.

Before the bud opens, it is covered with thin, pointy, green scales. These are the flower's **sepals**. The **sepals** protect the soft parts of the flower as they grow inside the bud.

The **sepals** are tough and hairy. They keep insects from eating the flower before it opens. When it is fully grown, the flower bud is as big as a chicken's egg.

The sunflower opens.

The flower opens on a warm, sunny day. It takes at least a day to open fully. Unlike many other flowers, a sunflower has both male and female parts in each flower head.

After four days, the male parts start to make **pollen**, and the female parts—called **stigmas**—make **nectar**. The **nectar** smells sweet and attracts insects. The sunflower's bright yellow color also gets the attention of insects.

The sunflower faces the sun.

Most sunflowers grow in warm, sunny parts of the world, often in large fields. Each sunflower is about 12 inches (30 cm) wide.

The big flowers need the warm sunlight to make **nectar**, so each flower turns to face the sun.
In a large field, all of the sunflowers will face the sun. They follow it as it slowly moves across the sky.

Insects visit the sunflower.

Bees, flies, crickets, and other insects visit the sunflower to feed on the sweet **nectar**. When they land on the flower, they get covered in sticky **pollen** from the male parts of the flower.

The insects carry the **pollen** to other sunflowers. As the insects land on the **stigmas**, **pollen** falls off the insects, and the **stigmas** are **fertilized**. When this happens, a seed begins to grow.

The sunflower makes seeds.

When all of the **stigmas** have been **fertilized**, the flower is no longer needed. Its petals dry up. The flower head hangs downward to keep rain from harming the growing seeds.

The plant keeps making food, which is stored in the growing seeds. By fall, the seeds are ready to **harvest**. Some will be eaten or crushed to make oil. Others will be planted next spring to grow new sunflowers.

Word bank

Fertilized - the female parts of a sunflower are fertilized when they come into contact with pollen from the male parts of a sunflower. This happens when insects move between sunflowers. Only a fertilized sunflower will make seeds.

Harvest - when people collect fully grown crops from fields or gardens.

Nectar - a sweet liquid made by the female parts of a sunflower. Nectar attracts bees and other insects.

Nutrients - substances in soil that help plants grow.

Pollen - a fine powder made by the male parts of a sunflower.

Seed leaves - the first leaves that grow on a plant. When larger leaves start to grow, seed leaves die.

Sepals - the outside part of a flower that protects the petals as they grow inside the flower bud.

Stigmas - the female parts of a flower that make nectar. When a stigma is fertilized by pollen, a seed starts to grow.

Veins - the tiny tubes in a leaf or stem that carry food and water around the plant.

Life cycle

Soon after planting, a root from the sunflower seed pushes down into the soil.

When the sunflower is fertilized, it makes seeds. Next spring, these can be planted to grow new sunflowers.

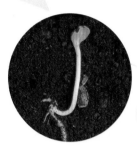

A few days later, the stem and seed leaves grow.

Soon after opening, the sunflower makes nectar. This attracts insects.

The seed leaves push to the surface and unfold.

About four weeks later, the sunflower opens.

A week later, larger leaves grow.

After eight weeks, the plant starts to grow a flower bud.

Index